Go Light Your World
By Kimberly Stringer
Illustrations by Debbie Fleck

Copyright 2022
All Rights Reserved

978-1-7379308-5-3

Published by Personal Chapters LLC

Carry your candle and show them how to cope.

Be a bright flame of Joy and Love for all to see.

So lend a hand, and give your heart.

God will save us, but we must do our part.

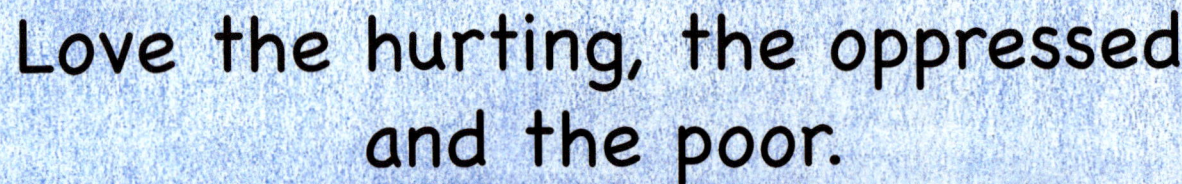
Love the hurting, the oppressed and the poor.

Go light your world with a flame so bright.

Peace, Love and Joy will fill the night.

A bright and burning flame...
your light will be a glorious ray!

Kreative Kids Academy students sharing their light...

 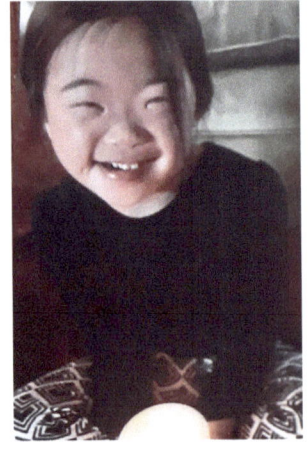  

   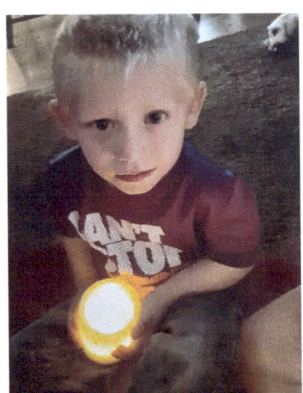

Students in Kreative Kids Academy are discovering their own light and learning how to share it with the world around them.

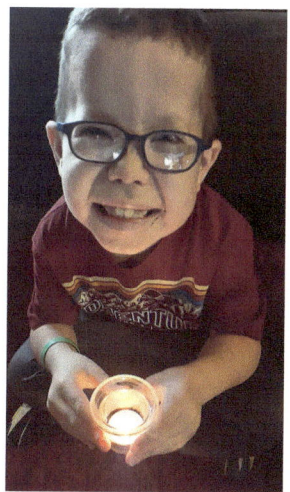

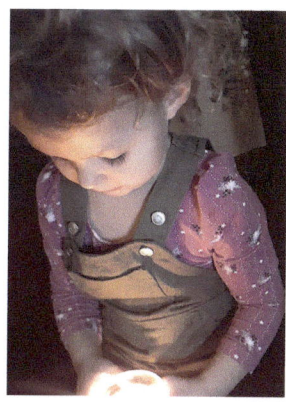

Other books by Kimberly Stringer:

Loving Lauren

Leonard the Leprechaun Plays Hide & Seek

Rocks in my Pocket

Bully Bully Blue Jay

I Swallowed a Bubble

About the Author and Illustrator

Author Kimberly Stringer has been an early childhood educator for more than 35 years. She has a strong belief that children need to be outside and she has specialized in an outdoor curriculum. She shies away from computer technology, preferring a more natural, science and ecology-based teaching methodology based on immersion in the great outdoors. Before the pandemic, she operated Kreative Kids in Wichita, KS as a pre-school, but has since opened up her private operation to ages three through grade five in Kreative Kids Academy. Mrs. Kim has always been creative in her use of books and storytelling and loves to feature her students in her books. She has numerous stories lined up and as long as she has students, she will never run out of books.

Illustrator Debbie Fleck's love for art began at an early age. Self-taught, her gift from God has led her along many paths and touched many people's lives. She has explored various mediums, including oil, acrylics, watercolor and pastels.

Kathy Troccoli has been sharing her light for decades through music and ministry

Kathy Troccoli* is enjoying almost four decades of ministry. Her passion has always been toward offering comfort and encouragement and she continues to do just that.

KT's numerous accolades include 24 recordings, 18 number-one radio hits, 19 Dove Award nominations, 2 Dove Awards, and 3 Grammy nominations. In addition to her success in Christian music she has made quite an impact in the mainstream arena as well, scoring a top charting hit with Everything Changes as well as a top 10 single with the iconic Beach Boys, entitled I Can Hear Music. She's just as comfortable singing her heart out in a stadium alongside Billy Graham to Pope John Paul—as she is belting out a big band tune or crooning her velvet voice on a jazz standard at the iconic Metropolitan Room in New York City.

Kathy, gifted singer—is also a songwriter, speaker, author and host.. From serving on the mission fields of Africa, China, India and Central America, to performing before millions—to hosting 20 years of rejuvenating and relaxing cruises, Kathy enjoys all aspects of using her gifts to entertain as well as embolden the spirit.

To share your light with the world, consider joining or donating to Kathy's foundation at ***www.golightyourworldfoundation.org***

*All images and references to Kathy Troccoli used with permission

www.ingramcontent.com/pod-product-compliance
Lightning Source LLC
Chambersburg PA
CBHW040017050426
42451CB00002B/21